Coloring with My ABC's

Illustrated
by
Savannah Skye

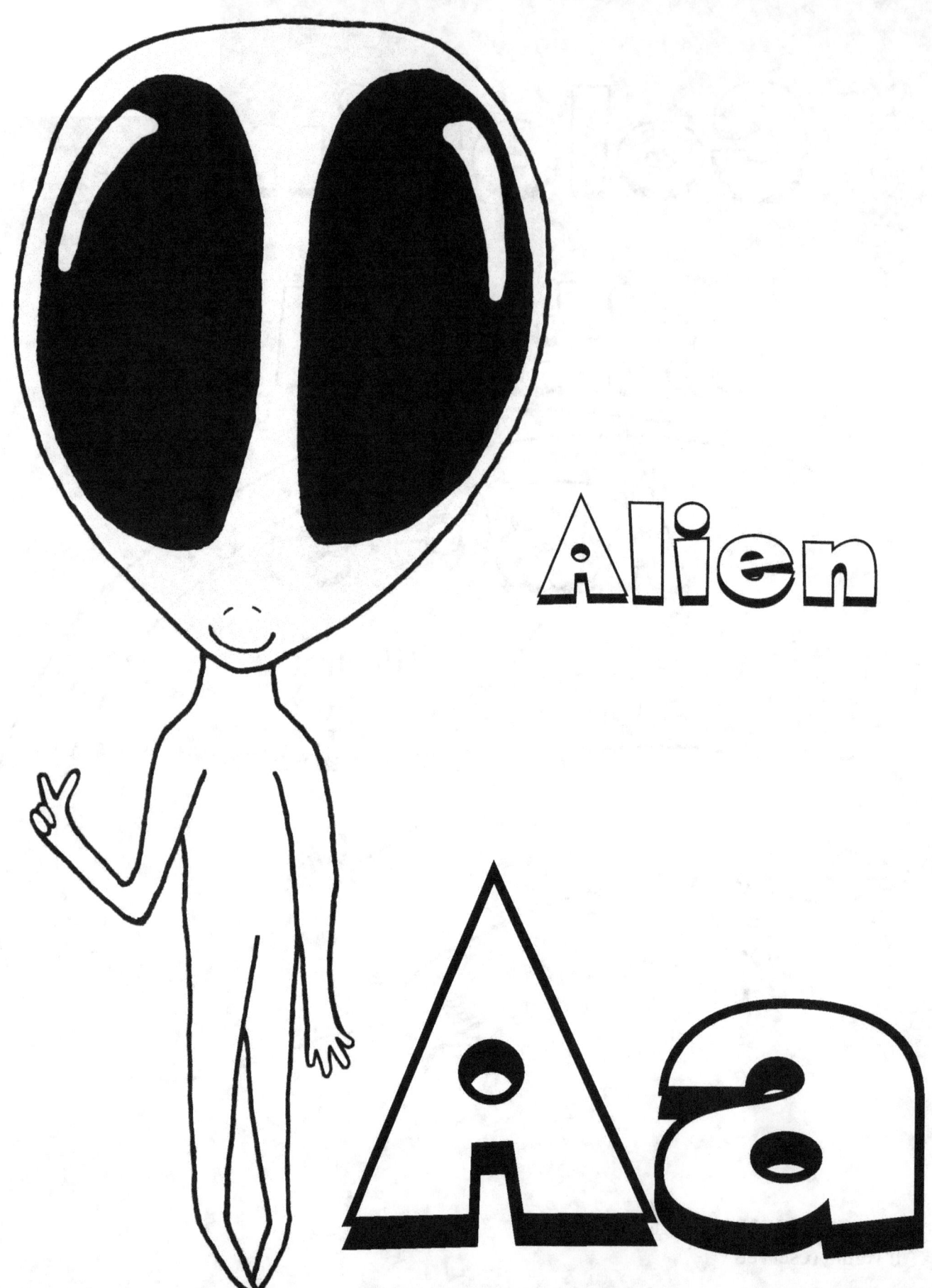

Alien

Aa

Bee

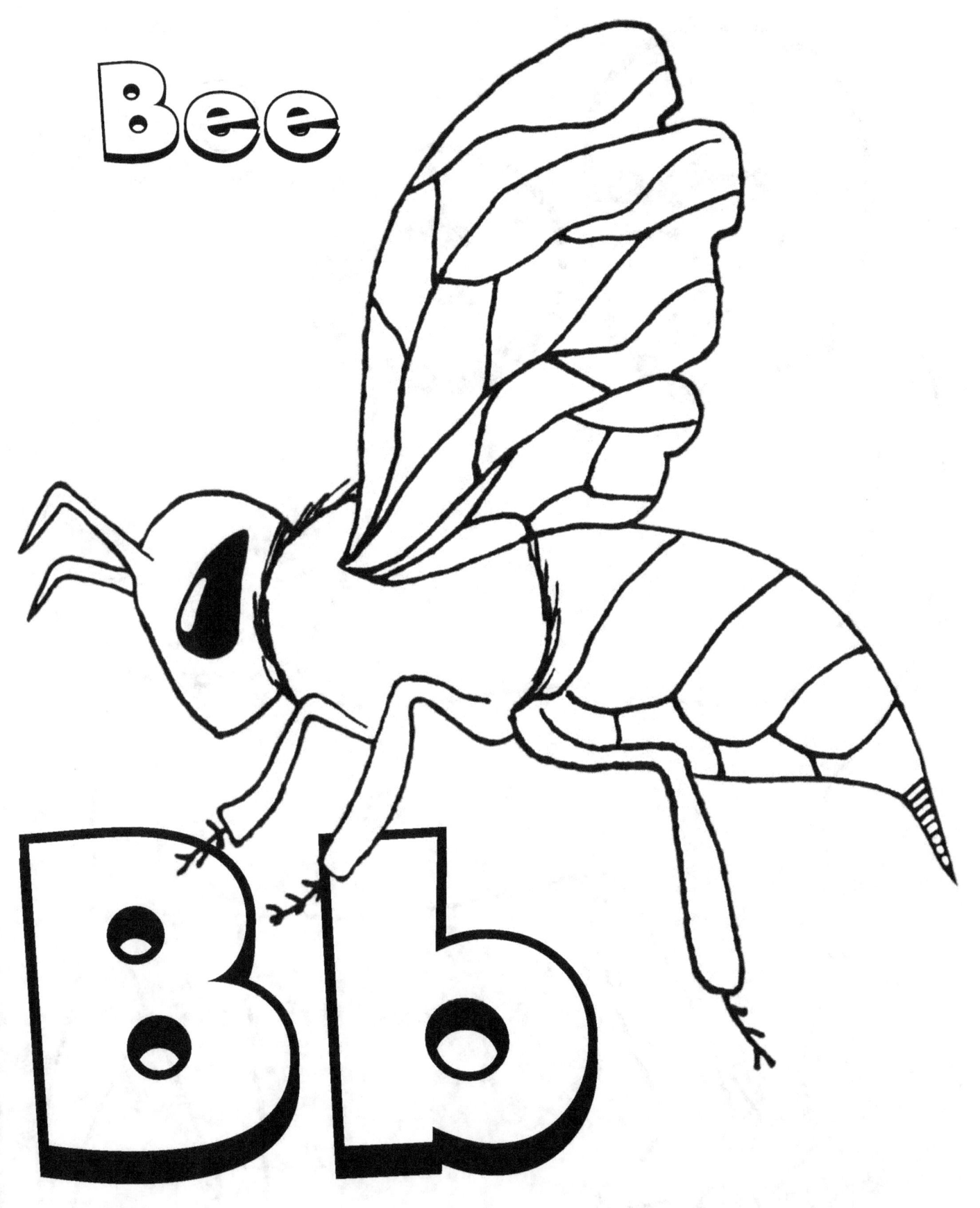

Bb

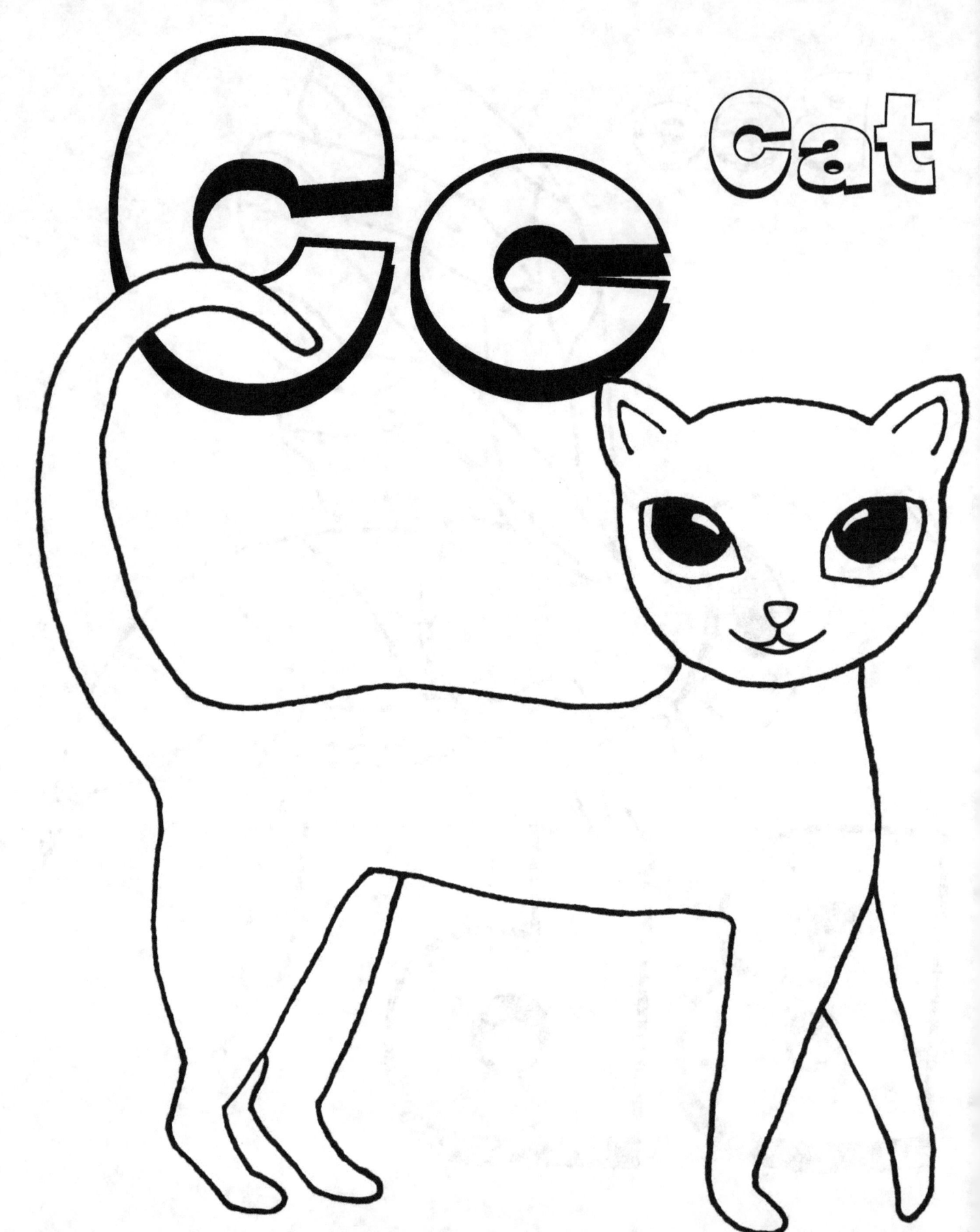

Cc Cat

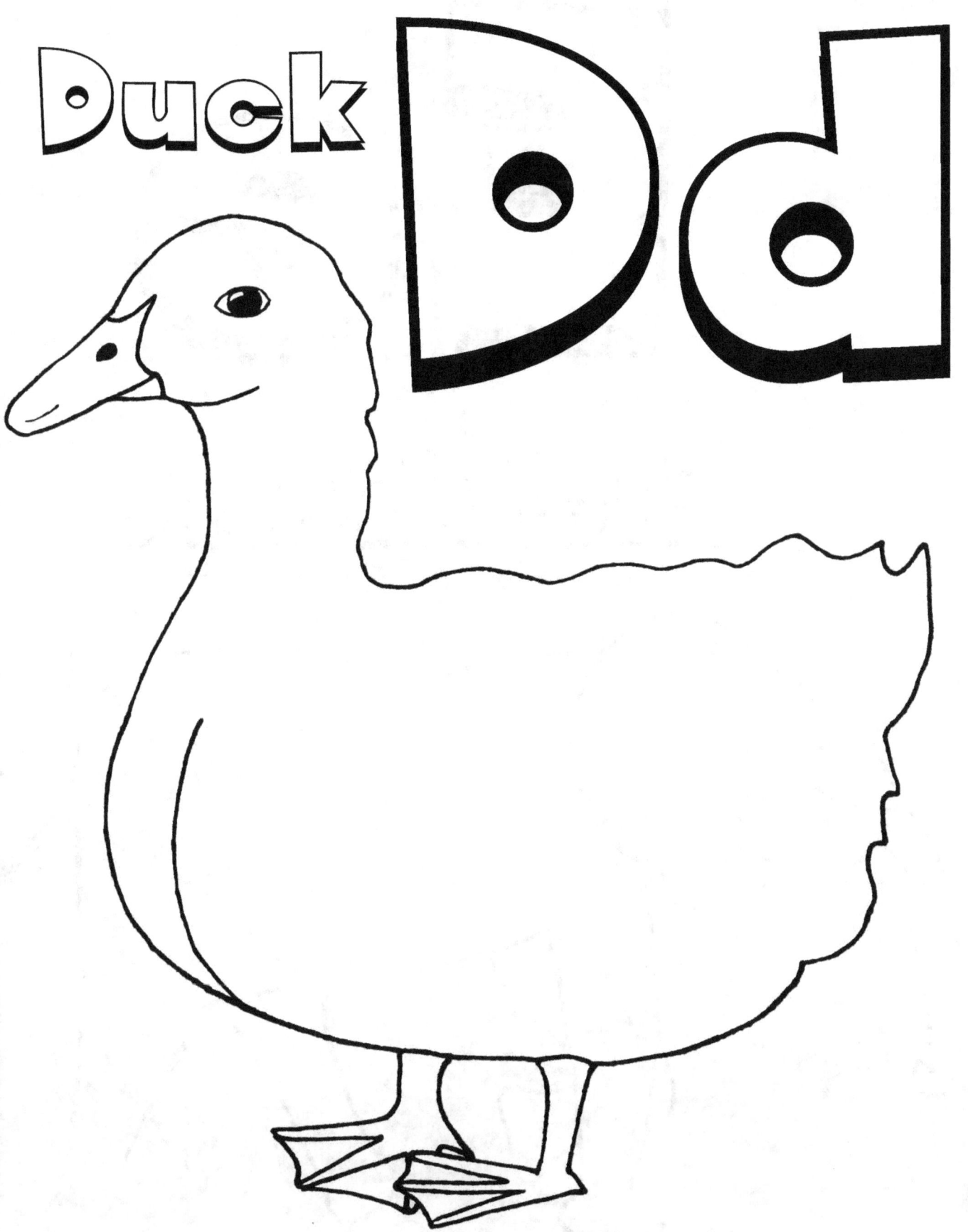

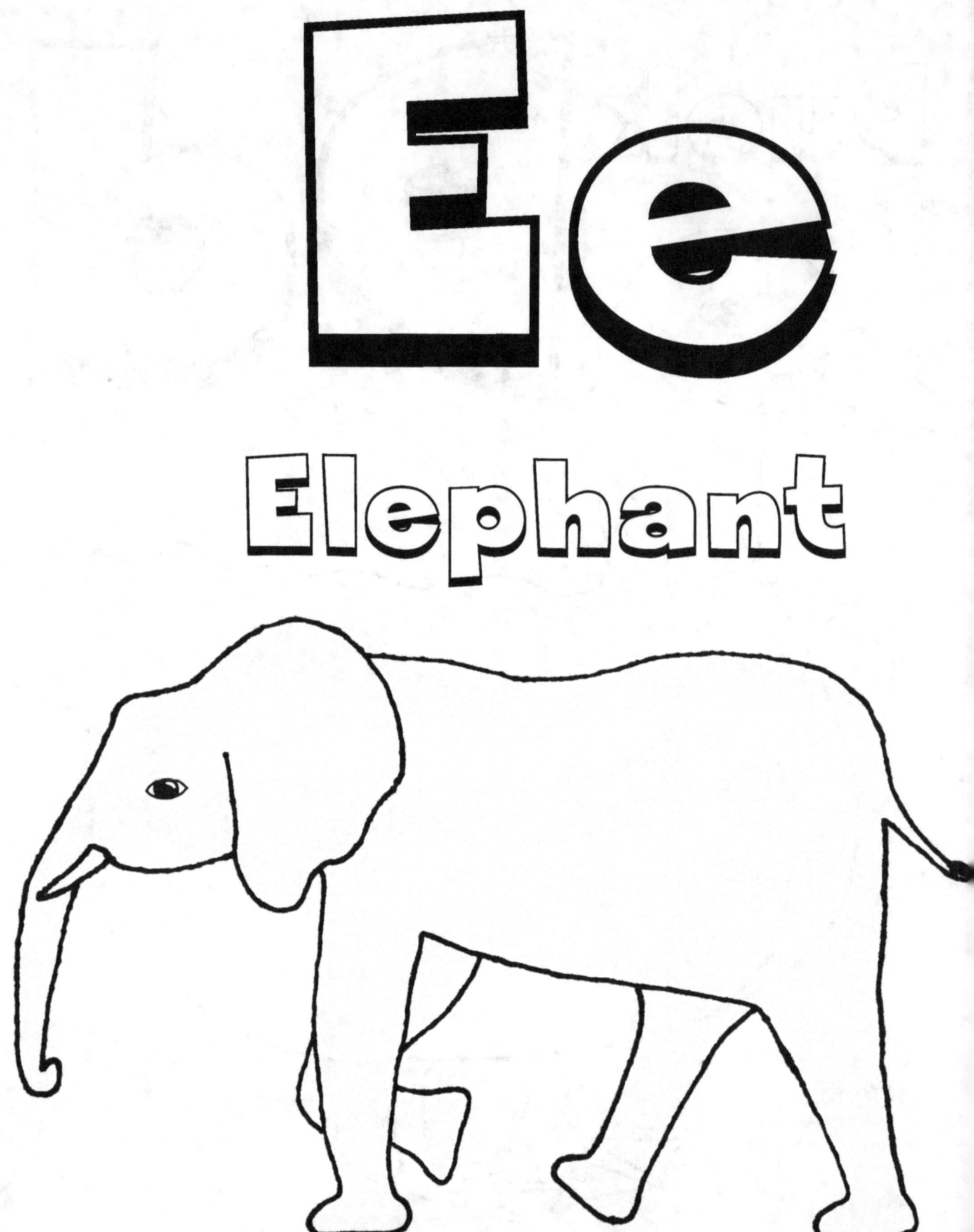

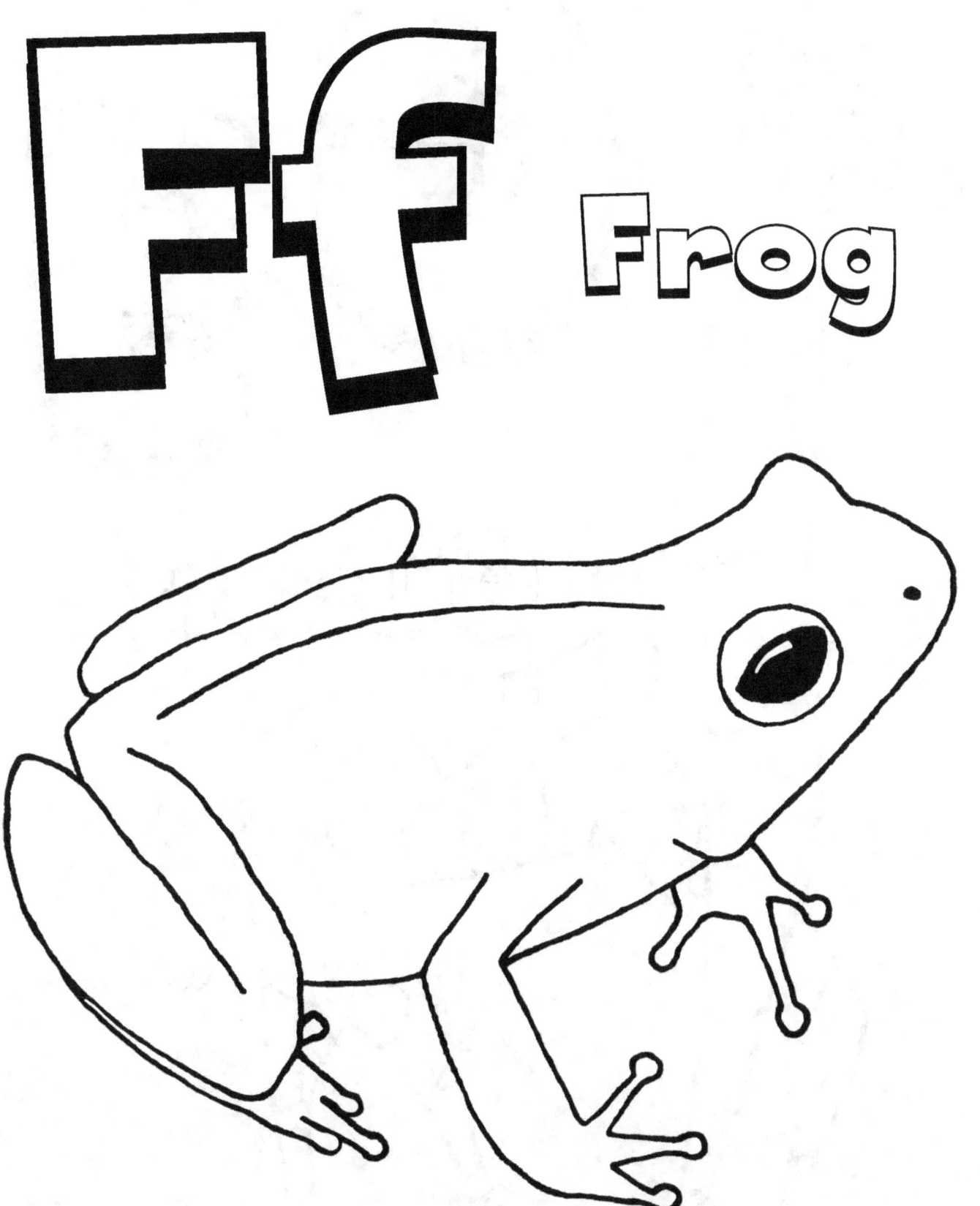

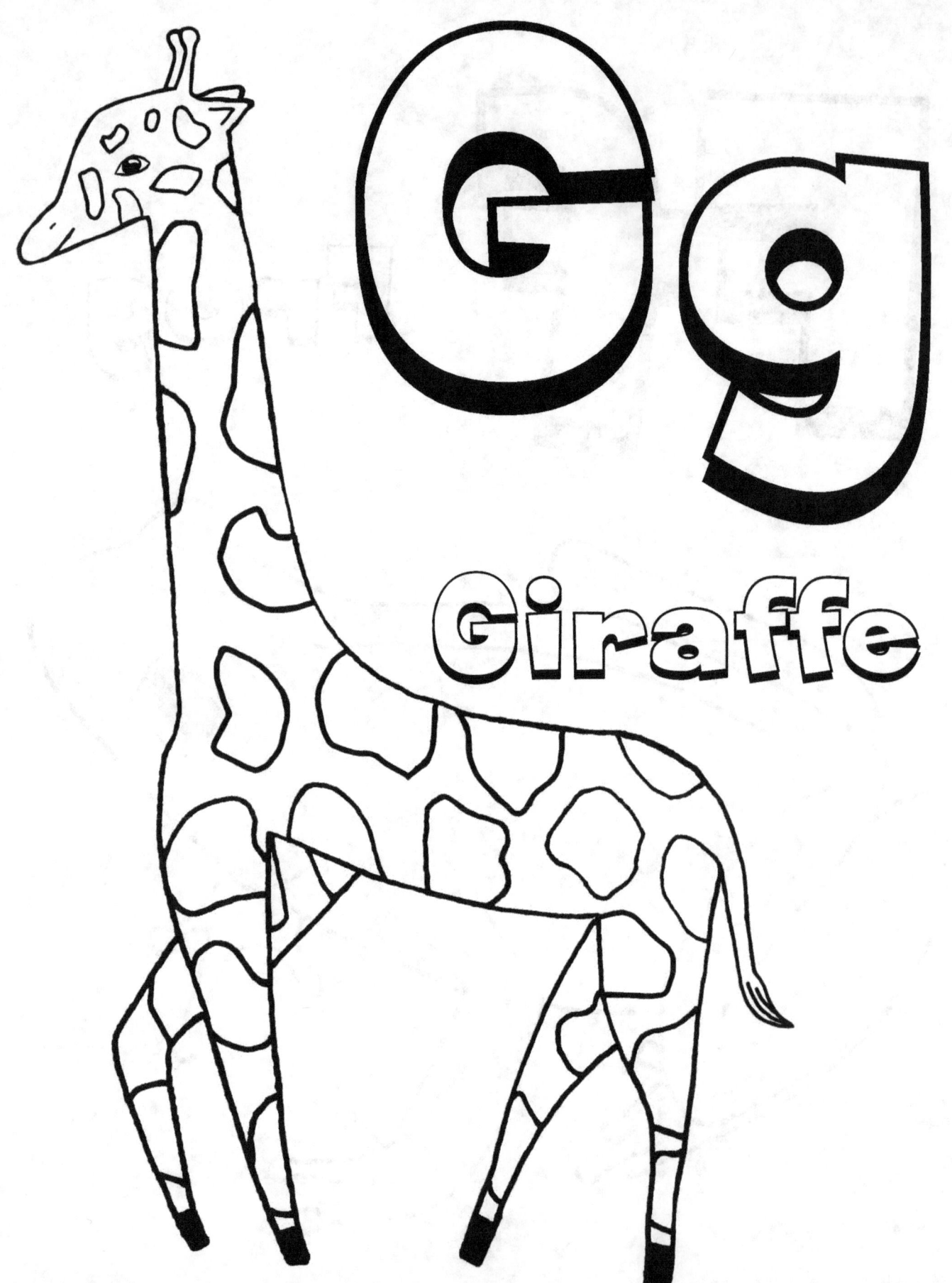

Gg

Giraffe

Hh

Horse

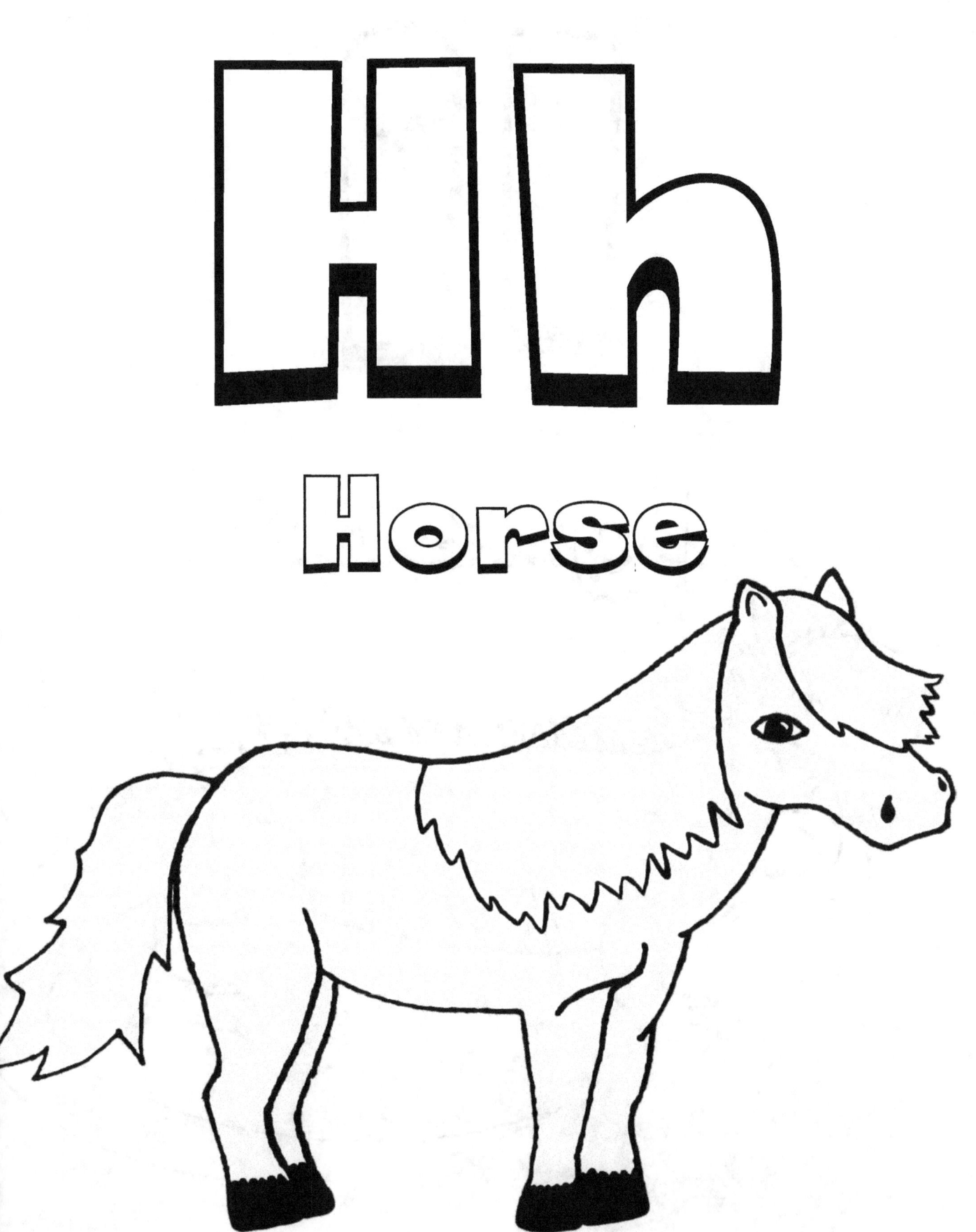

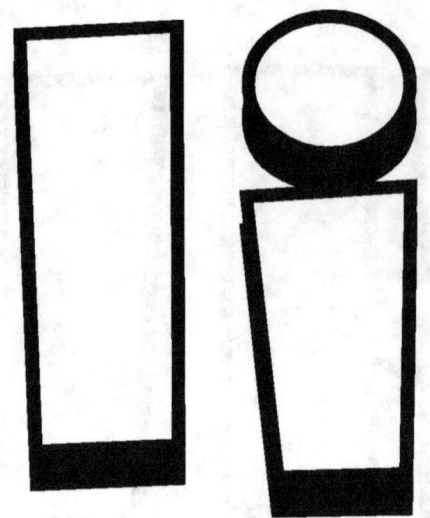

Iguana

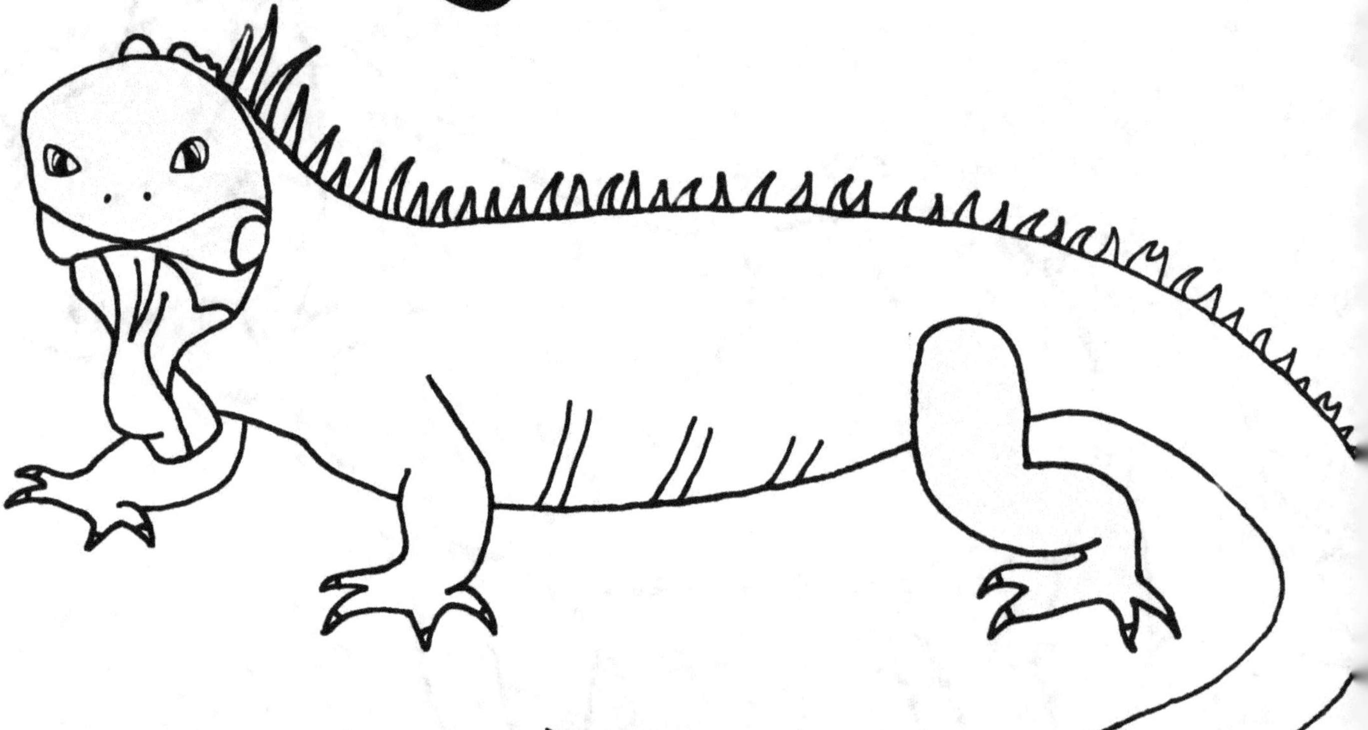

Jj Jackal

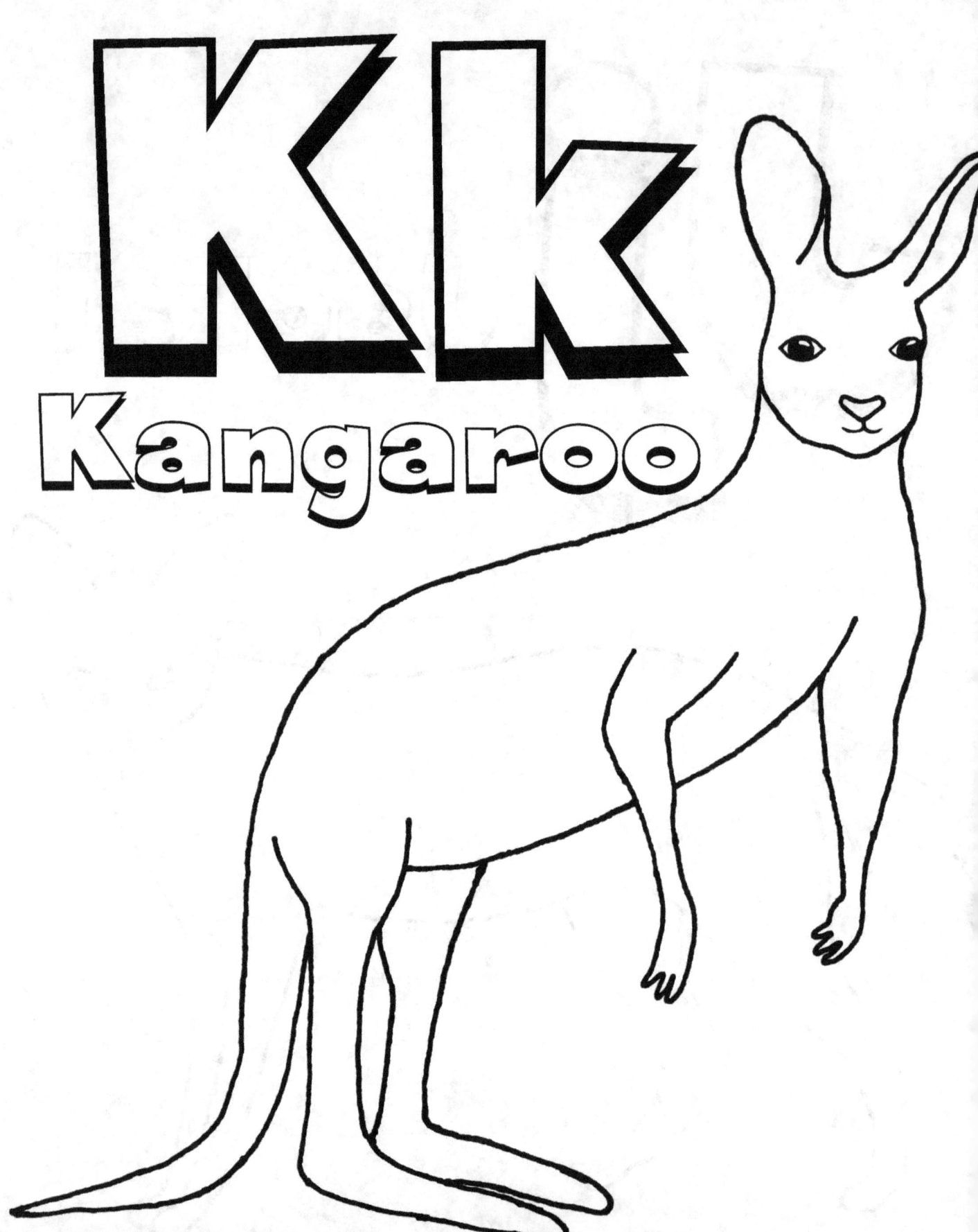

Ll

Lizard

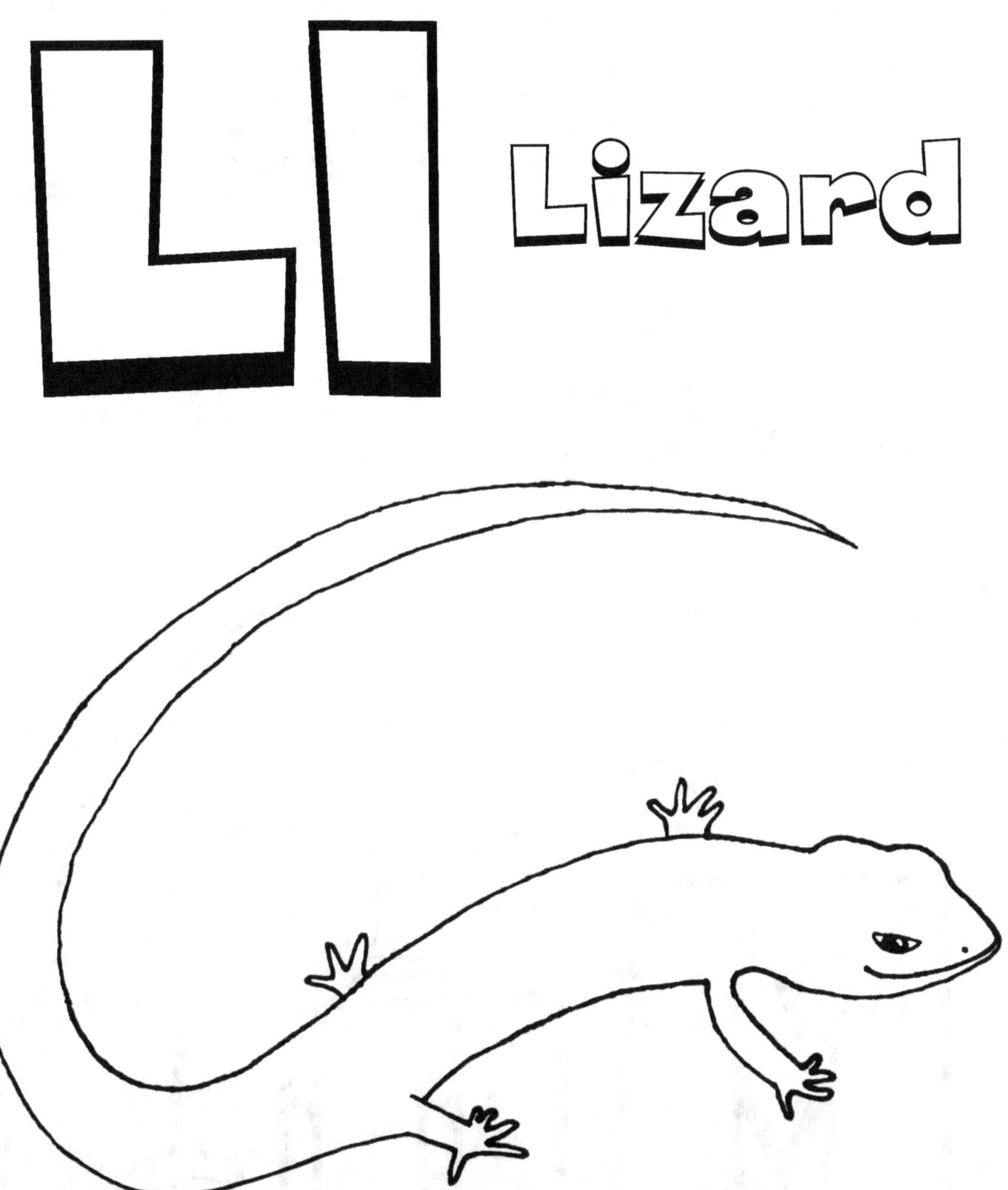

Mouse

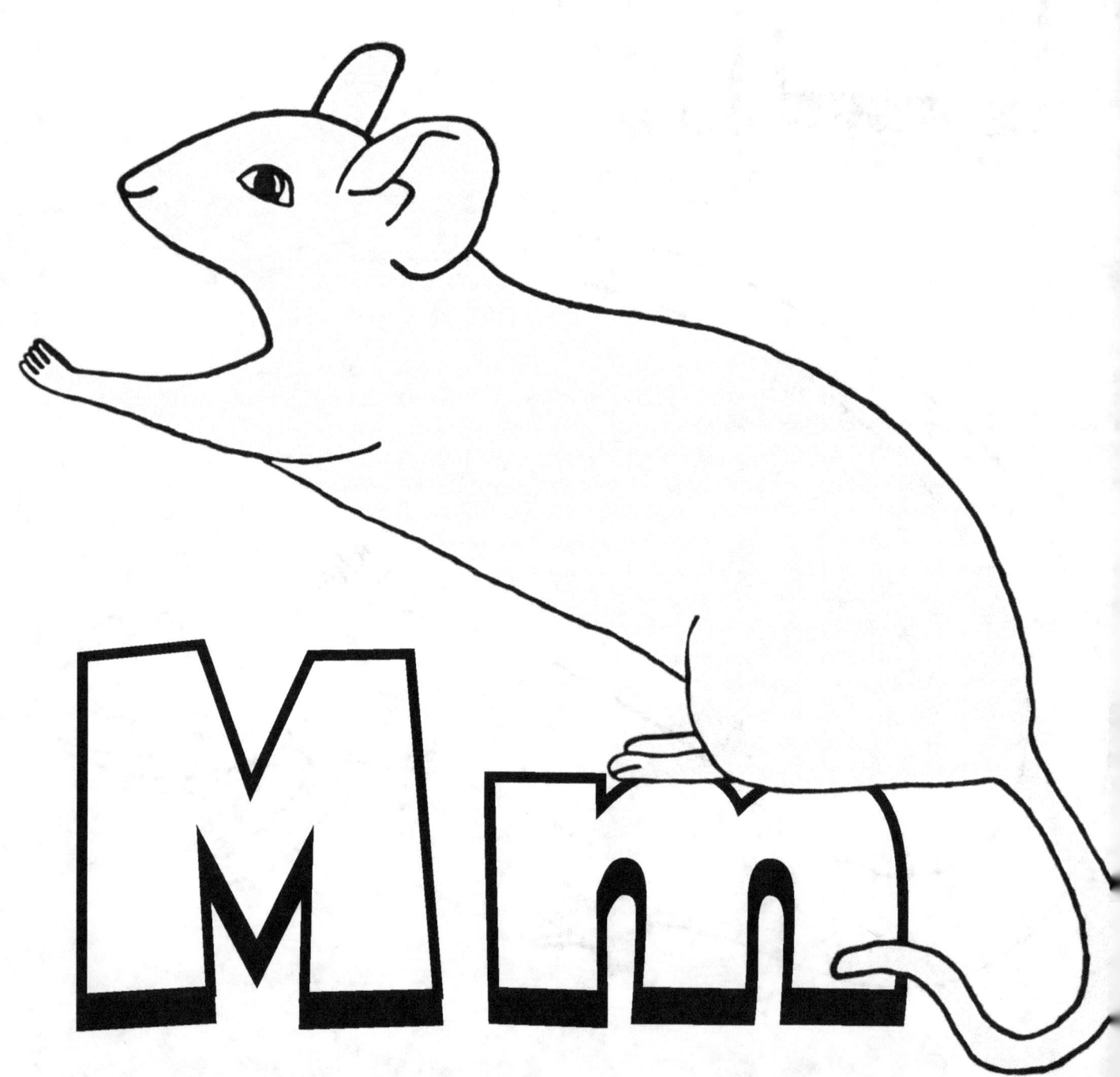

M m

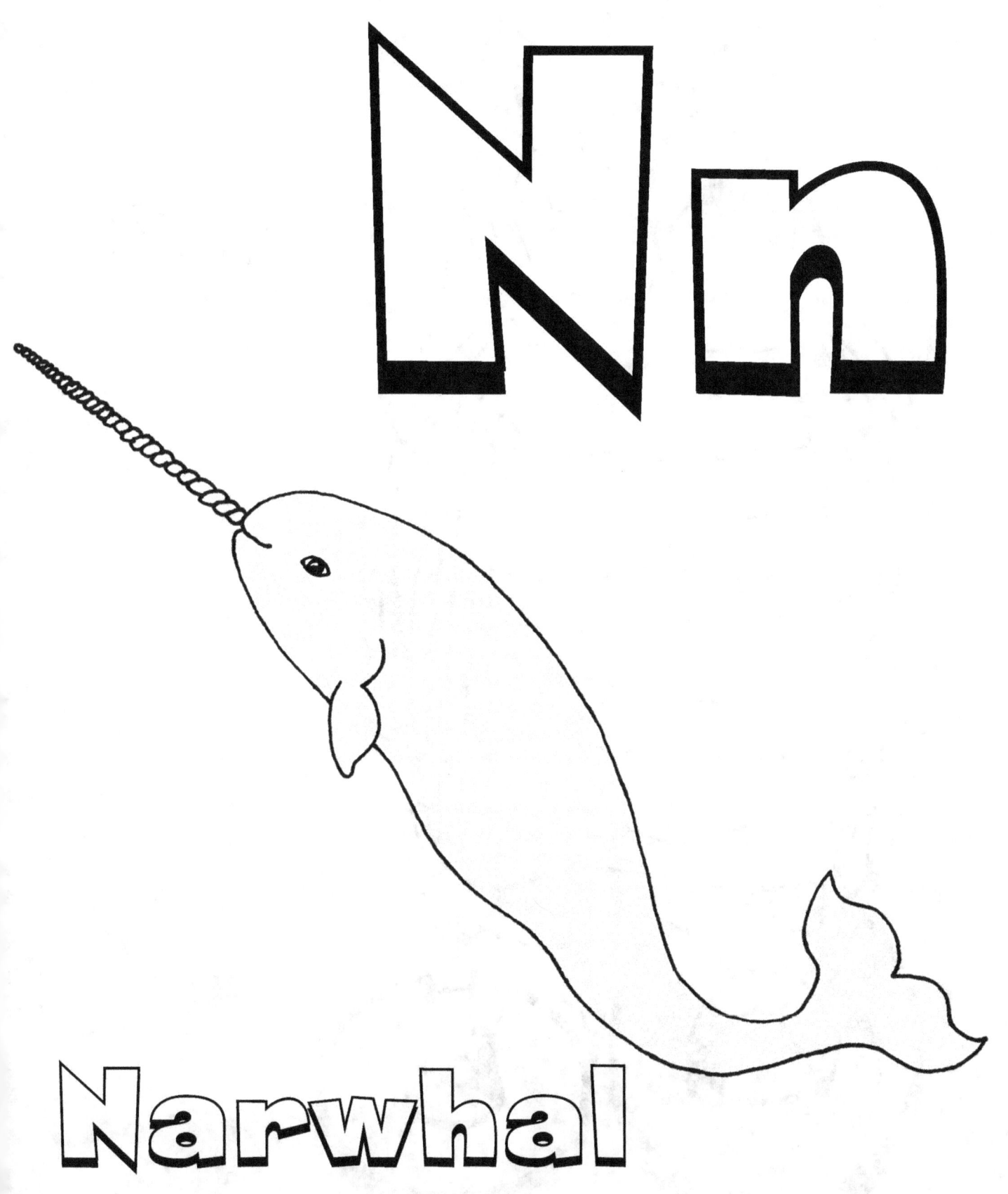

Narwhal

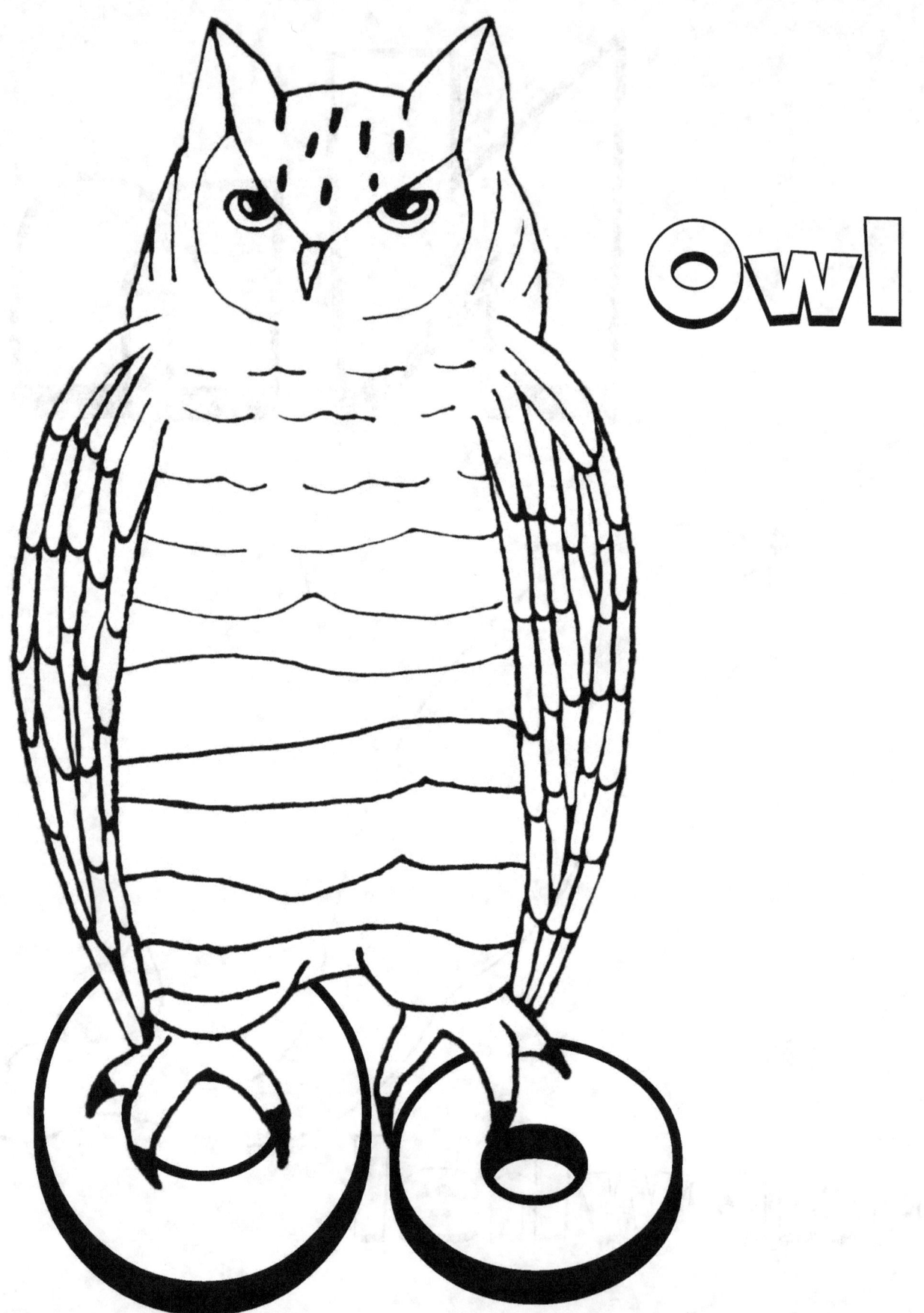

Penguin

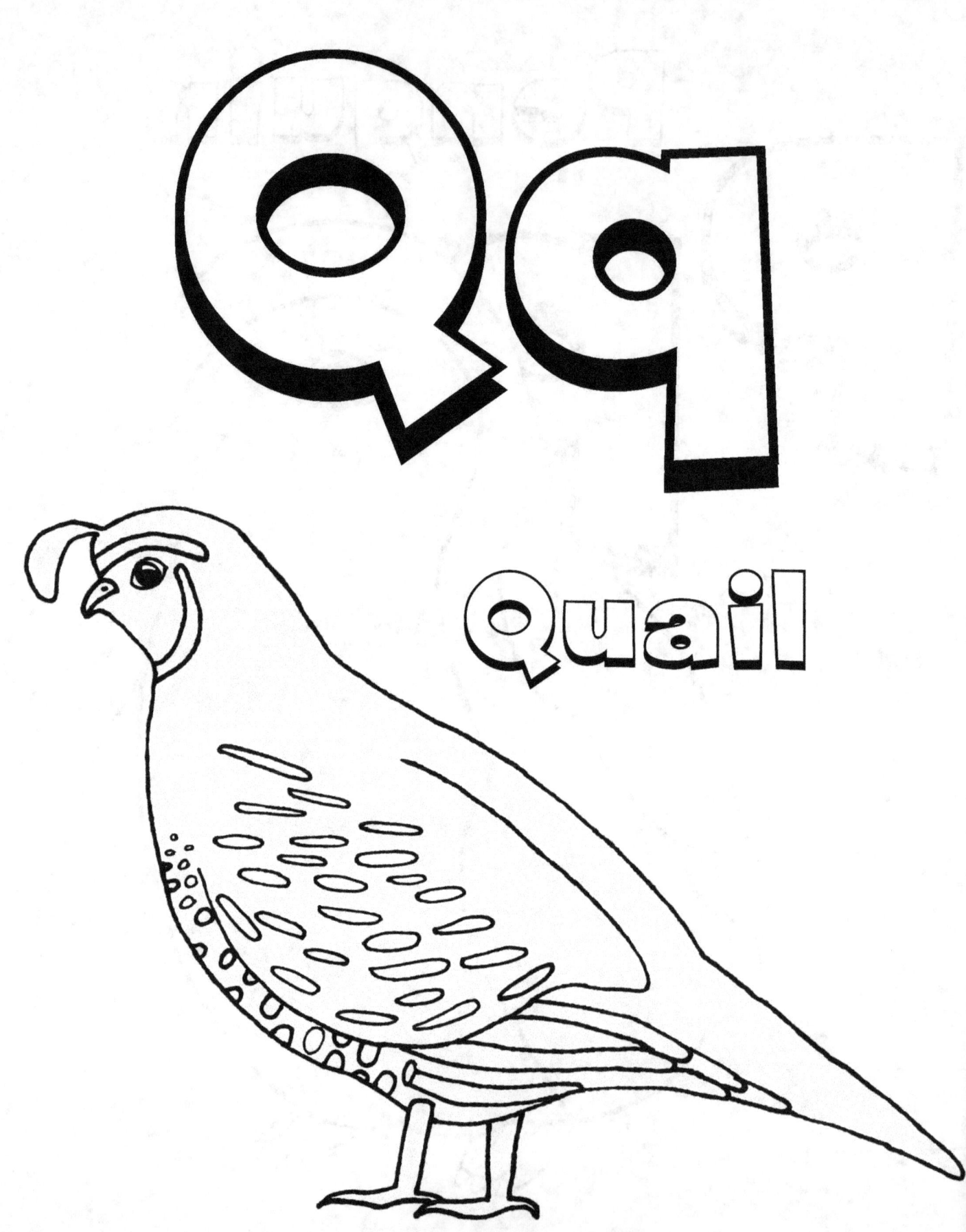

Quail

Rr

Rabbit

Ss

Squirrel

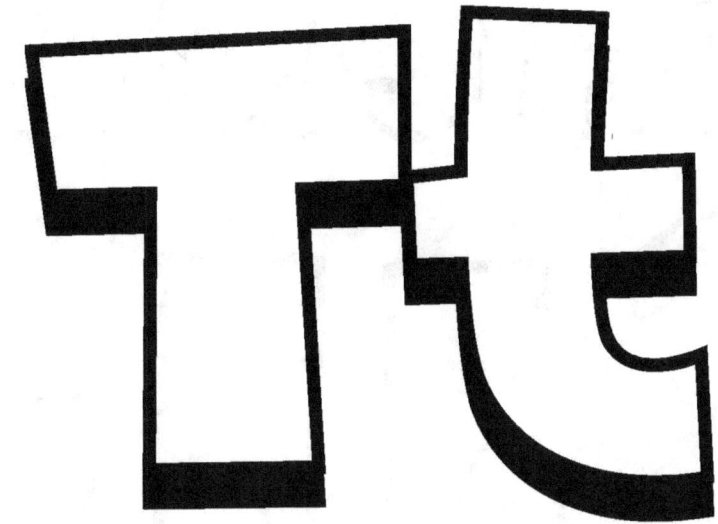

Turtle

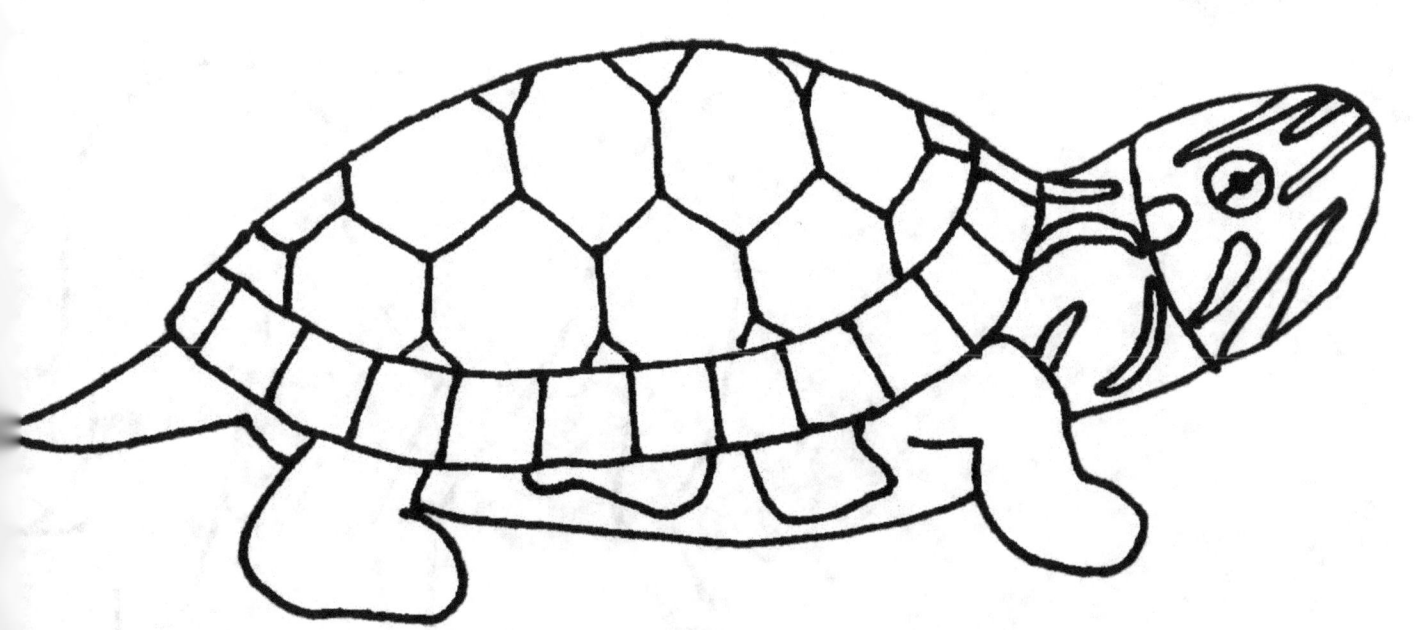

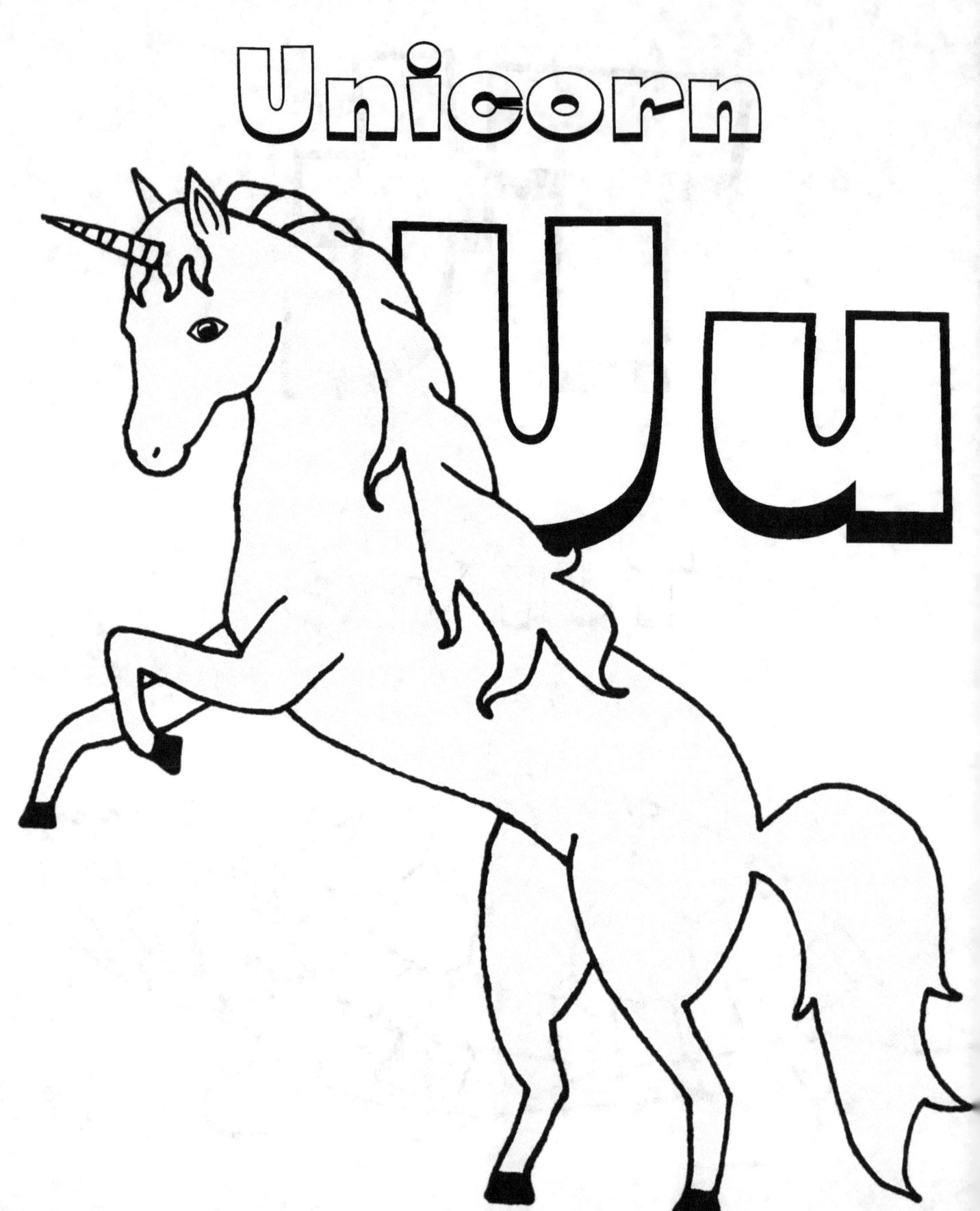

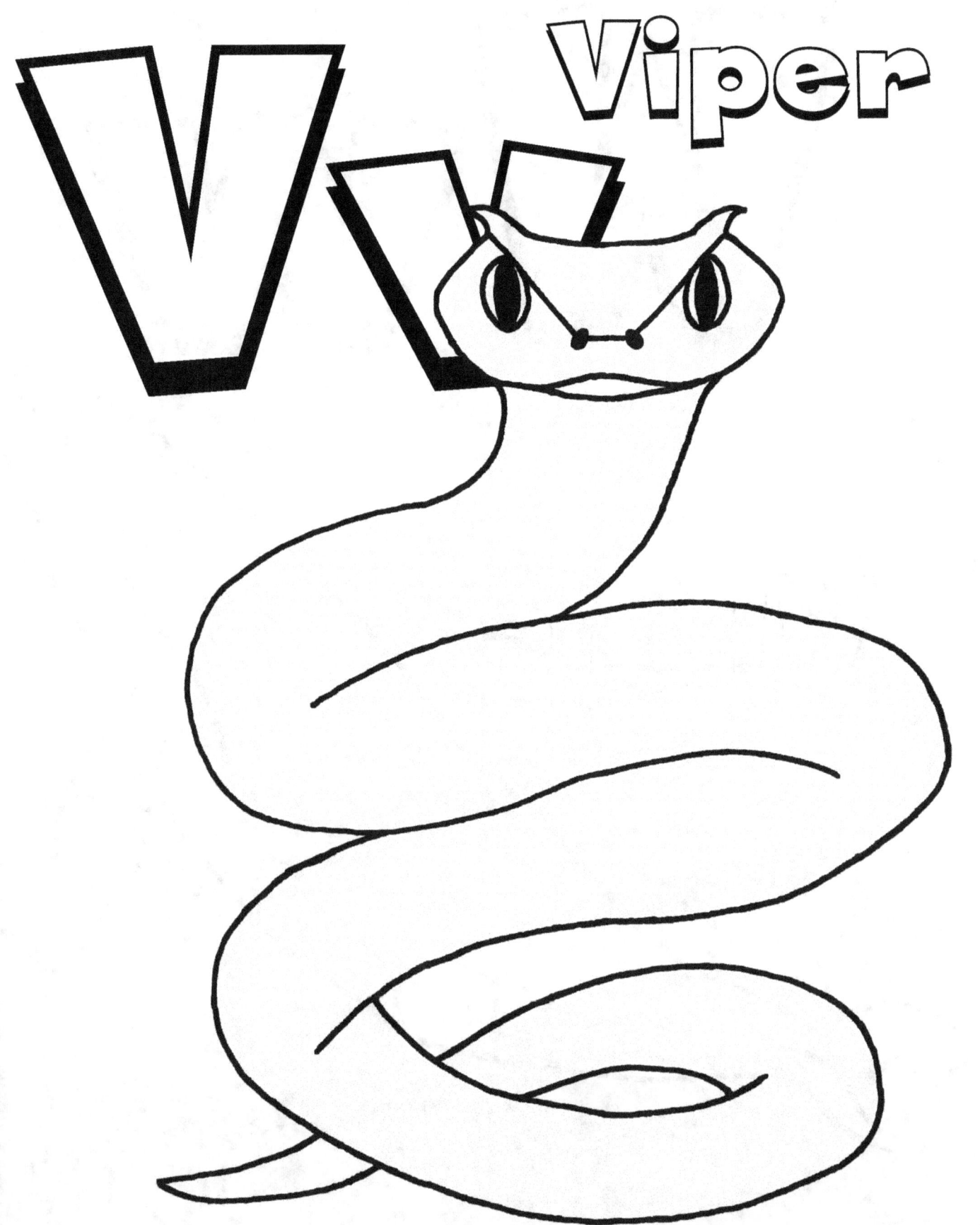

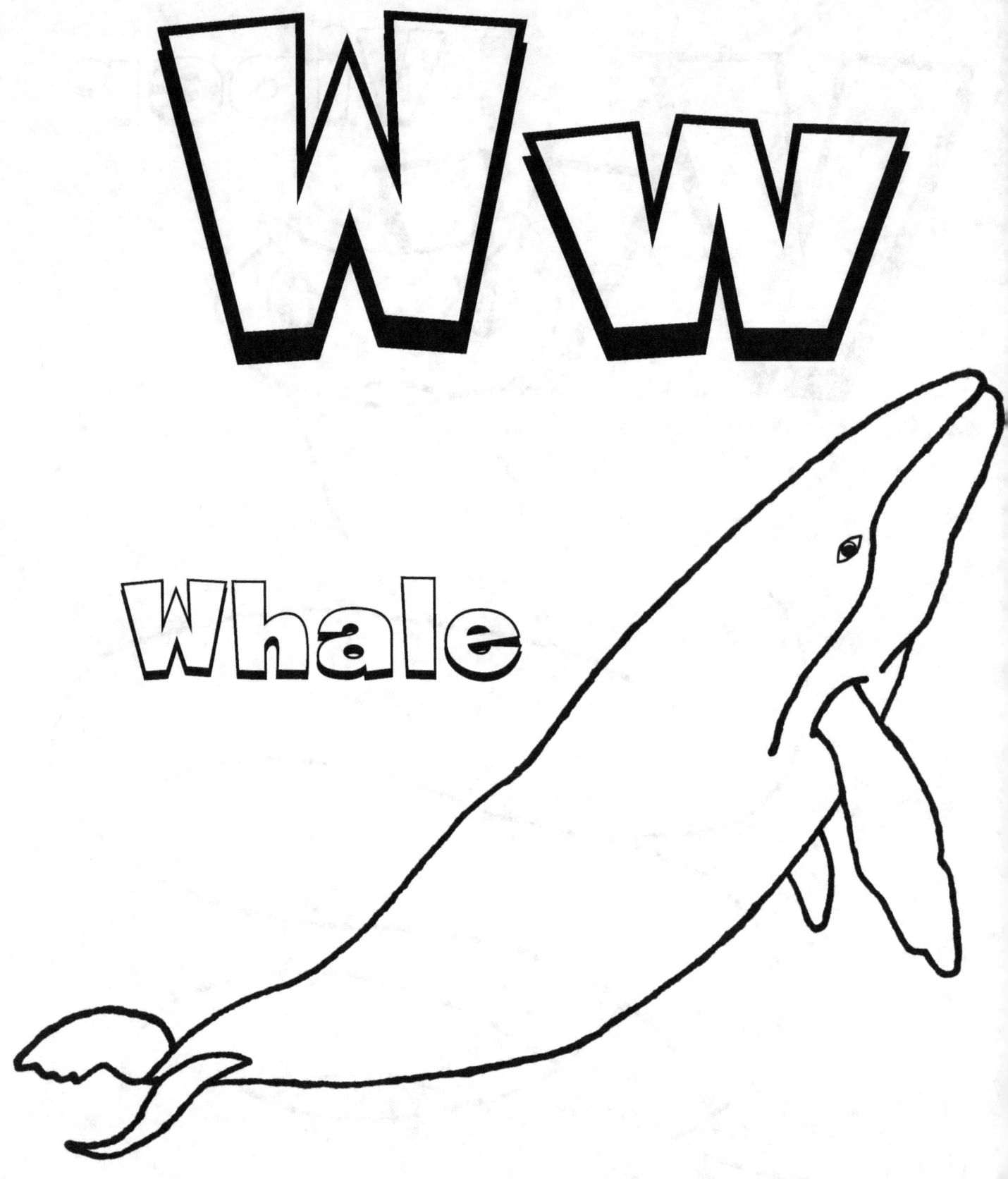

Xx

X-Ray

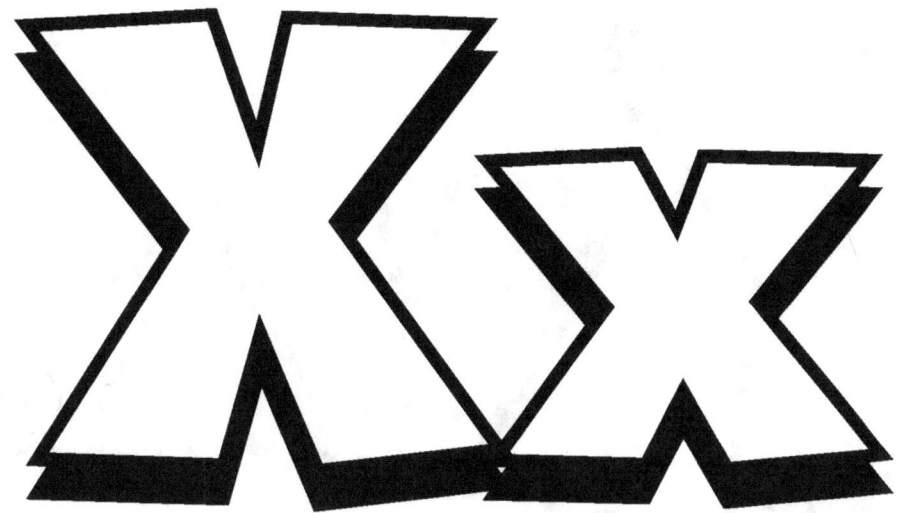

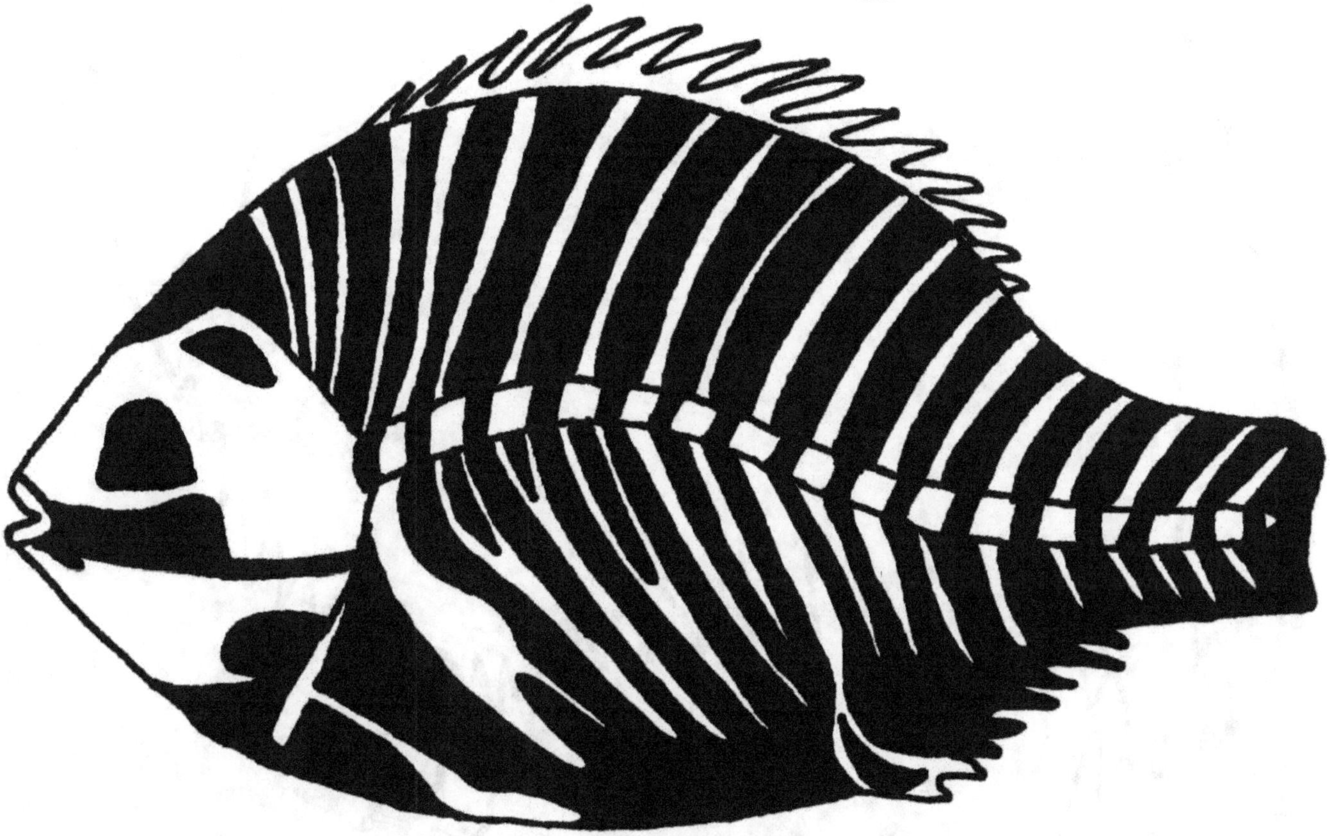

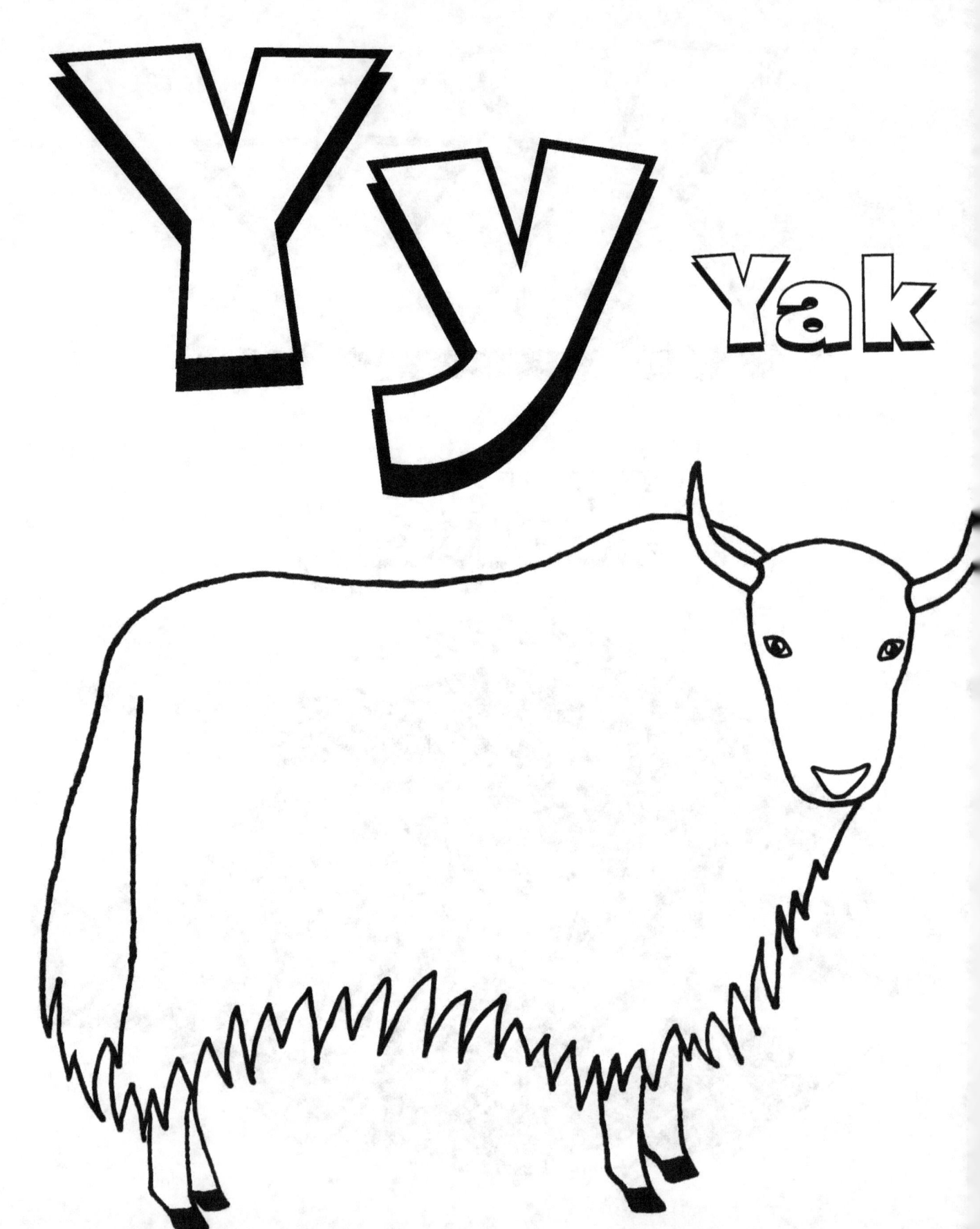

Yy Yak

Zz

Zebra

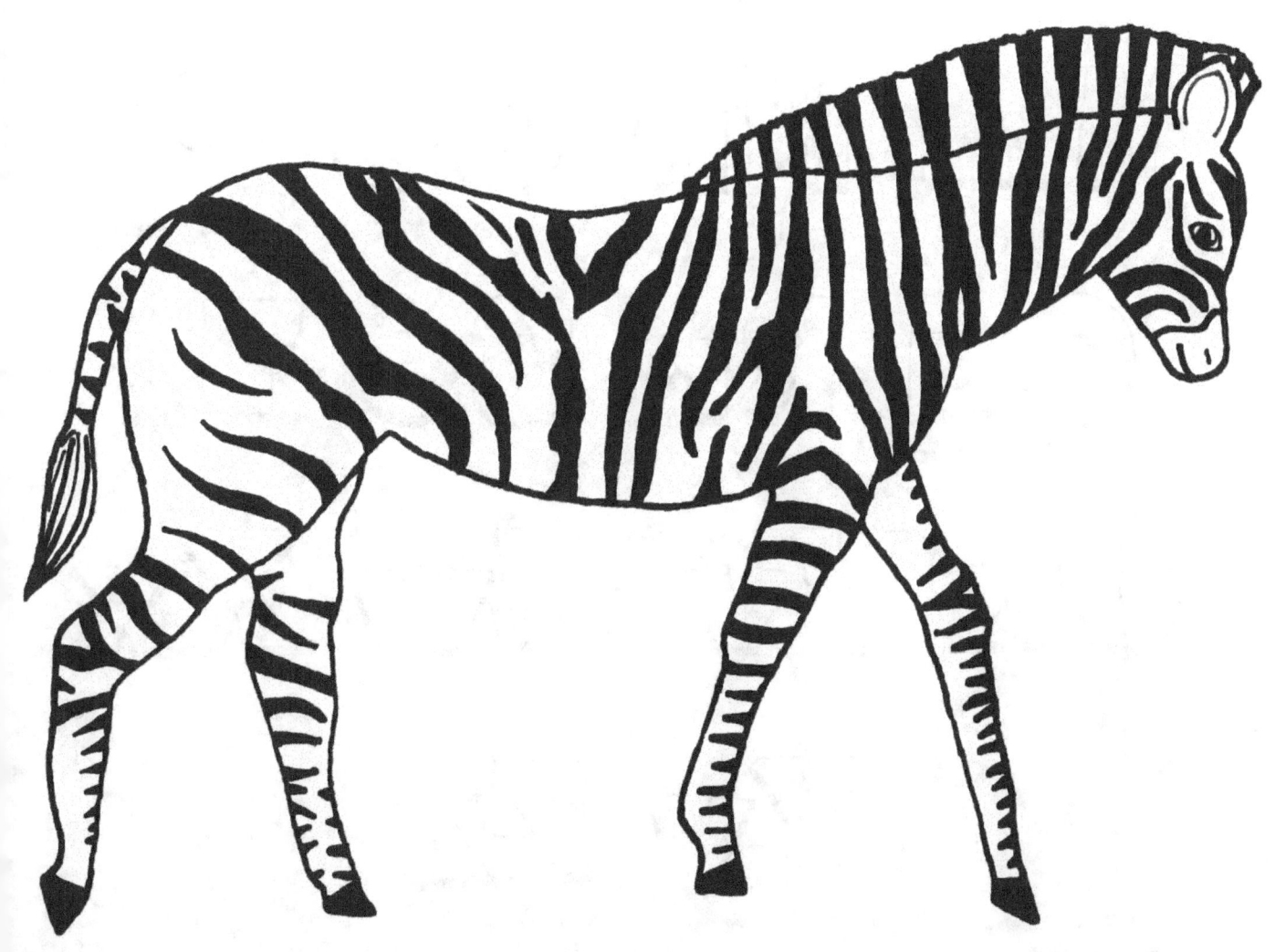

Aa Bb Cc Dd

Ee Ff Gg Hh

Ii Jj Kk Ll

Mm Nn Oo Pp

Qq Rr Ss Tt

Uu Vv Ww Xx

Yy Zz

Available Now!

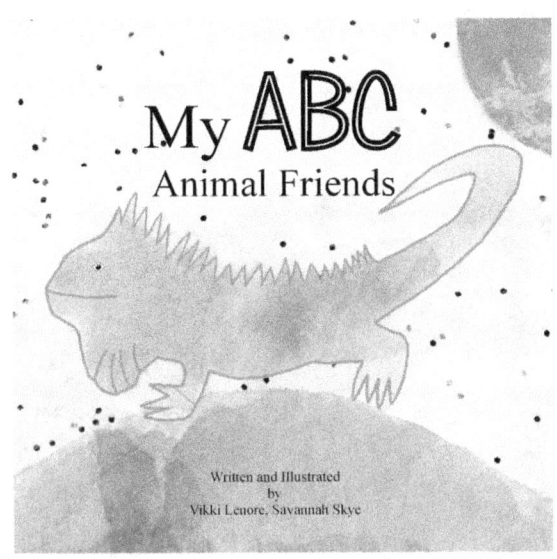

My ABC
Animal Friends

Written and Illustrated
by
Vikki Lenore, Savannah Skye

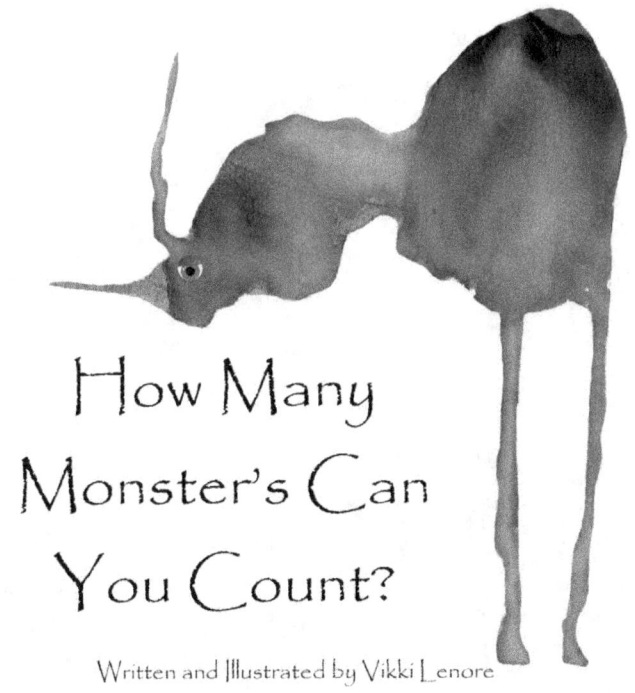

How Many
Monster's Can
You Count?

Written and Illustrated by Vikki Lenore

www.ingramcontent.com/pod-product-compliance
Lightning Source LLC
Chambersburg PA
CBHW081624220526
45468CB00010B/3019